First Class Reader!

Integrated Skills Lessons for Beginners

Sharron Bassano
Santa Cruz City Schools

with
John Duffy

Nancy Kirk
Illustrator

ALTA BOOK CENTER PUBLISHERS
14 Adrian Court, Burlingame, California 94010 USA

Project Editor: John M. Duffy
Copyeditors: Marc Lecard, Dan Kapelovitz

Design/Production: E. Carol Gee
Additional Art: C. Buck Reynolds

acc 03/01

Printed in the United States of America

ALTA BOOK CENTER PUBLISHERS—SAN FRANCISCO

14 Adrian Court
Burlingame, California 94010 USA
Phone: 800 ALTA/ESL • 650.692.1285
Fax: 800 ALTA/FAX • 650.692.4654
Email: info@altaesl.com
Website: WWW.ALTAESL.COM

ISBN 1-882483-29-4

I dedicate this book
to my mother, *Kay Hudson.*

Special thanks to Rachel Harris
for her inspired editing and
suggestions for improvement
of the final draft.

Thank you to Nancy Kirk
for the delightful drawings
that make these lessons truly
comprehensible.

Contents

Contents – *continued*

1. Eleni Is from Italy

A

name
Eleni
Italy

lives
United States

address
219 Front Street
Jackson, CA 94551

telephone number
555-3971

social security number
987-65-4320

is working
restaurant
daytime
waitress

is going
school
at night

is studying
English

not married
single

1. _____ 2. _____ 3. _____

4. _____ 5. _____ 6. _____

Eleni Is from Italy

Her name is Eleni.

She is from Italy.

She lives in the United States now.

Her address is 219 Front Street, Jackson, CA 94551.

Her telephone number is 555-3971.

Her social security number is 987-65-4320.

She is working in a restaurant in the daytime.

She is a waitress.

She is going to school at night.

She is studying English.

She is not married. She is single.

Questions and Answers

		Questions	Answers
1.		What is her name? Where is she from?	Her name is Eleni. She's from Italy.
2.		What is her address?	Her address is 219 Front Street, Jackson, CA 94551.
3.		Is she working in a restaurant?	Yes, she is.
4.		Is she going to school at night?	Yes, she is.
5.		Is she married?	No, she's single.

Write about the Picture

1. Her name is Eleni.
   She is from Italy.

2.

3.

4.

Interaction Grid

Permission is granted to make one photocopy of this page in order to do
*the **Interaction Grid** activity and to avoid cutting the page.*

Match the Words and Pictures   D

address   waitress   school   daytime
telephone number   restaurant   studying English   at night

1. _studying English_

2. _____

3. _____

4. _____

5. _____

6. _____

Write about Yourself

1. What is your name?

_____

2. What is your address?

_____
number   street   apt number

_____
city   state   zip code

2. Tomas Is from Mexico

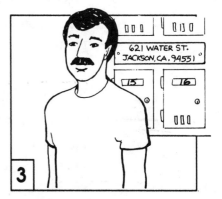

name
Tomas
Mexico

lives
United States

address
621 Water Street
Apt. 15
Jackson, CA 94551

telephone number
555-1279

social security number
987-65-4325

is working
factory
at night
assembler

is going
school
daytime

is studying
English

married
no children

1. _____ 2. _____ 3. _____

4. _____ 5. _____ 6. _____

Tomas Is from Mexico

His name is Tomas.

He is from Mexico.

He lives in the United States now.

His address is 621 Water Street, Apt. 15, Jackson, CA 94551.

His telephone number is 555-1279.

His social security number is 987-65-4325.

He is working in a factory at night.

He is an assembler.

He is going to school in the daytime.

He is studying English.

He is married. He has no children.

Questions and Answers

		Questions	Answers
1.		What is his name? Where is he from?	His name is Tomas. He's from Mexico.
2.		Where does he live?	He lives in the United States now.
3.		Is he working in a factory in the daytime?	No, he's working at night.
4.		Is he going to school in the daytime?	Yes, he is.
5.		Is he married or single?	He's married.

Write about the Picture

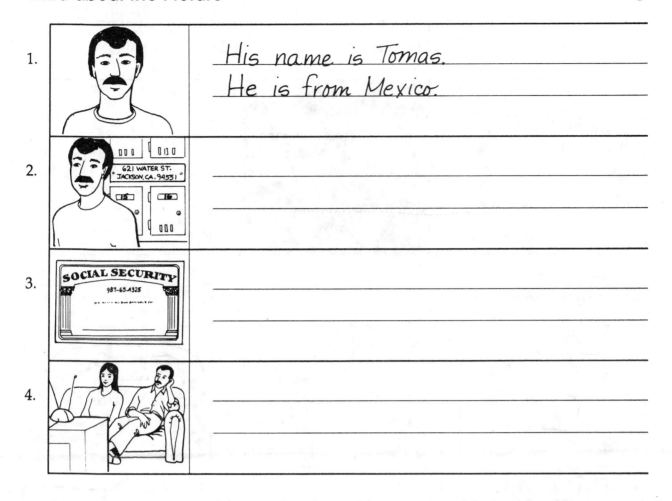

1. His name is Tomas.
   He is from Mexico.

2.

3.

4.

Interaction Grid

Match the Words and Pictures

factory	telephone number	married	daytime
assembler	social security number	single	at night

1. *social security number*

2. _____

3. _____

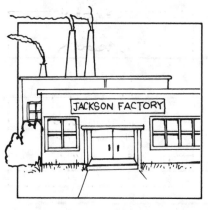

4. _____

5. _____

6. _____

Write about Yourself

1. Where are you from?

_____

2. When do you go to school?

_____

3. Mrs. Lim and Mr. Pappas

1

Mrs. Lim
China

2

Mr. Pappas
Greece

3

work
high school
teachers

4

Mrs. Lim
short
four feet ten inches tall

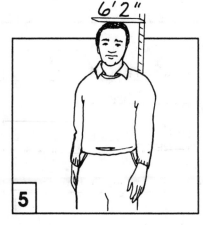

5

Mr. Pappas
tall
six feet two inches tall

98 lbs.

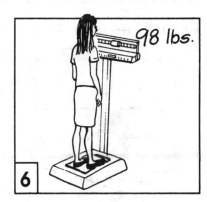

6

slender
weighs
98 pounds

210 lbs.

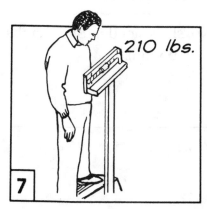

7

heavy
weighs
210 pounds

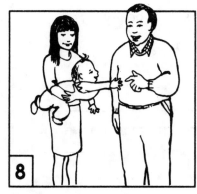

8

Mrs. Lim
married
girl

9

Mr. Pappas
single

1. _____   2. _____   3. _____

4. _____   5. _____   6. _____

Mrs. Lim and Mr. Pappas

Mrs. Lim is from China.

Mr. Pappas is from Greece.

They work in the high school. They are teachers.

Mrs. Lim is short. She is four feet ten inches tall.

Mr. Pappas is tall. He is six feet two inches tall.

Mrs. Lim is slender. She weighs 98 pounds.

Mr. Pappas is heavy. He weighs 210 pounds.

Mrs. Lim is married. She has a baby girl.

Mr. Pappas is single.

Questions and Answers

	Questions	Answers
1.	Is Mrs. Lim short?	Yes, she is. She's four feet ten inches tall.
2.	Is Mr. Pappas tall?	Yes, he is. He's six feet two inches tall.
3.	Is Mrs. Lim heavy?	No, she's slender. She weighs 98 pounds.
4.	Is Mrs. Lim married?	Yes, she is.
5.	Is Mr. Pappas married?	No, he's single.

Write about the Picture

1.	4'10"	<u>Mrs. Lim is short.</u> <u>She is four feet ten inches tall.</u>
2.	6'2"	
3.	98 lbs.	
4.	210 lbs.	

Interaction Grid

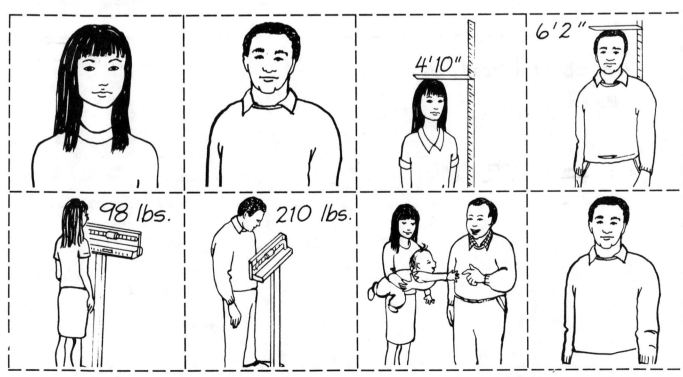

Match the Words and Pictures

D

tall	heavy	married	girl
short	slender	single	boy

1. _single_

2. _____

3. _____

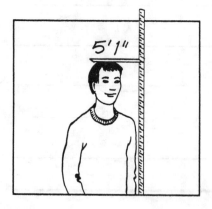

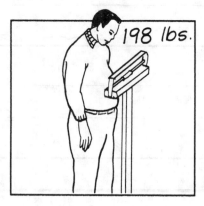

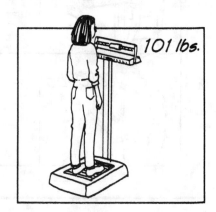

4. _____

5. _____

6. _____

Write about Yourself

1. How tall are you?

_____

2. Are you married or single?

_____

4. Friends

1

Mahmood
Iran

2

is working
garage
mechanic

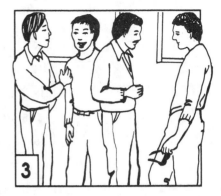

3

friends

4

are playing
cards
tonight

5

friend
Chen Li
TV repairman
repair shop

6

friend
Tomas
assembler
factory

7

Dan
computer operator
office

8

good
friends

9

like to
play cards
Friday night

1. _____   2. _____   3. _____

4. _____   5. _____   6. _____

4. Friends

This is Mahmood. He is from Iran.

He is working in a garage. He is a mechanic.

These are Mahmood's friends.

They are playing cards tonight.

His friend Chen Li is a TV repairman.

He is working in a repair shop.

His friend Tomas is an assembler.

He is working in a factory.

His friend Dan is a computer operator.

He is working in an office. They are good friends.

They like to play cards every Friday night.

Questions and Answers

		Questions	Answers
1.		Is Mahmood working in a garage? What's his occupation?	Yes, he is. He's a mechanic.
2.		Where is Chen Li working? What's his occupation?	He's working in a repair shop. He's a TV repairman.
3.		Where is Tomas working? What's his occupation?	He's working in a factory. He's an assembler.
4.		Where is Dan working? What's his occupation?	He's working in an office. He's a computer operator.
5.		Are they working tonight?	No, they're playing cards.

Write about the Picture

1. These are Mahmood's friends.

2.

3.

4.

Interaction Grid

Match the Words and Pictures

computer operator   TV repairman   assembler   mechanic
office   repair shop   factory   garage

1. *computer operator*   2. _____   3. _____

4. _____   5. _____   6. _____

Write about Yourself

1. What is your occupation?

_____

2. Where are you working?

_____

16

5. Neighbors

A

1

Mr. Chaam
lives
233 Wood Street

2

Mr. and Mrs. Wilson
live
235 Wood Street

3

Ms. Fulana and baby
live
apartment
237 Wood Street

4

neighbors
friends

5

Sunday
beautiful
sunny
day

6

Mr. Chaam
is working
vegetable garden

7

Mr. and Mrs. Wilson
are cooking
hamburgers

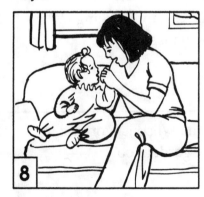

8

Ms. Fulana
baby
are playing

9

neighbors
are eating
dinner

1. _____ 2. _____ 3. _____

4. _____ 5. _____ 6. _____

Neighbors

Mr. Chaam lives at 233 Wood Street.

Mr. and Mrs. Wilson live at 235 Wood Street.

Ms. Fulana and her baby live in an apartment at 237 Wood Street.

They are neighbors and friends.

It is Sunday.

It is a beautiful, sunny day.

Mr. Chaam is working in his vegetable garden.

Mr. and Mrs. Wilson are cooking hamburgers on the barbecue.

Ms. Fulana and her baby are playing.

Now all the neighbors are eating dinner together.

Questions and Answers

	Questions	Answers
1.	Are they neighbors?	Yes, they are.
2.	Is it raining?	No, it's a beautiful, sunny day.
3.	Is Mr. Chaam working in the house?	No, he's working in the vegetable garden.
4.	Are the Wilsons working in the garden too?	No, they're cooking hamburgers on the barbecue.
5.	What is Ms. Fulana doing?	She's playing with her baby.

18

Write about the Picture

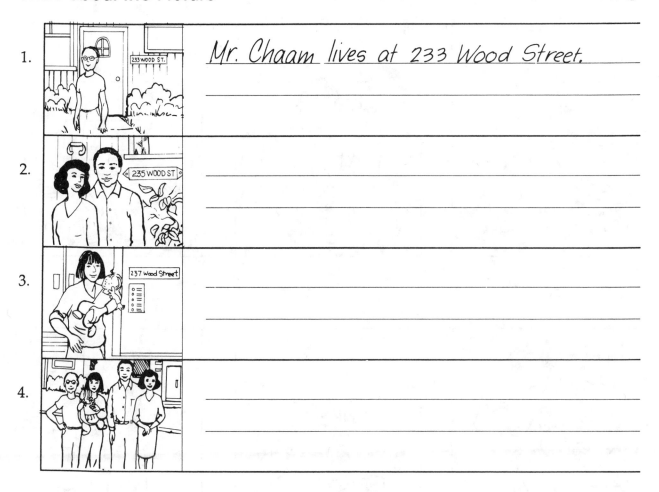

1. *Mr. Chaam* lives at 233 Wood Street.

2.

3.

4.

Interaction Grid

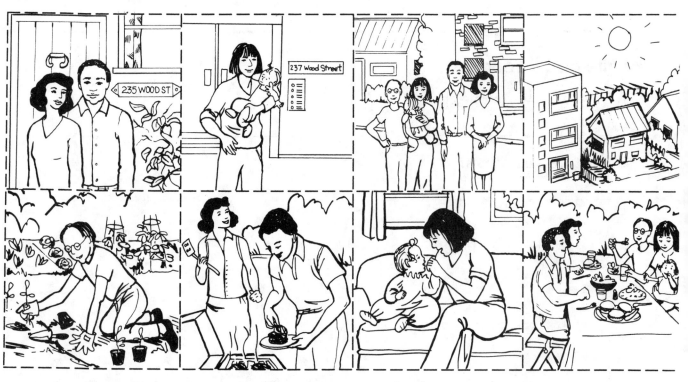

Match the Words and Pictures   D

cooking   playing   neighbors   sunny
eating   talking   live   in the garden

1. *in the garden*

2. _____

3. _____

4. _____

5. _____

6. _____

Write about Yourself

1. Do you know your neighbors?

_____

2. What are their names?

_____

6. Susana's Birthday

A

Susana
16 years old

today
birthday

at home
friends
family

are singing
Susana
Happy birthday to you

Susana
is blowing out
candles

mother
is cutting
cake

family
friends
are dancing

are talking
are laughing

Susana
is opening
presents

1. _____   2. _____   3. _____

4. _____   5. _____   6. _____

Susana's Birthday

B

This is Susana. She is 16 years old.

Today is her birthday.

She is at home with her friends and family.

They are singing to Susana:

> *Happy birthday to you, happy birthday to you,*
>
> *Happy birthday dear Susana, happy birthday to you.*

Susana is blowing out the candles.

Her mother is cutting the cake.

Her friends and family are dancing.

They are laughing and talking.

Susana is opening presents.

Questions and Answers

		Questions	Answers
1.		How old is Susana?	She's 16 years old.
2.		Is today her birthday?	Yes, it is.
3.		Where is she?	She's at home with her friends and family.
4.		What are they doing?	They're talking and laughing.
5.		What is Susana doing?	She's opening presents.

22

1.

This is Susana.
She is 16 years old.

2.

3.

4.

Interaction Grid

Match the Words and Pictures

blowing out candles   laughing   singing   birthday
cutting the cake   dancing   opening presents   family

1. _blowing out candles_

2. _____

3. _____

4. _____

5. _____

6. _____

Write about Yourself

1. When is your birthday?

_____

2. How old are you?

_____

7. Going to School

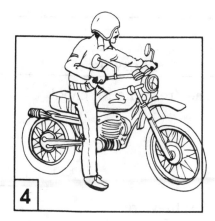

1

today
Monday

2

students
are going
school

3

Eleni and Susana
are riding
bicycles

4

Tomas
is riding
motorcycle

5

Chen Li
is driving
car

6

Mr. Pappas
is walking

7

Mahmood and Ms. Fulana
are taking
bus

8

Dan
very
tired

9

is not going
school
sleeping

1. _____ 2. _____ 3. _____

4. _____ 5. _____ 6. _____

Going to School

Today is Monday.

All the students are going to school.

Eleni and Susana are riding their bicycles.

Tomas is riding a motorcycle.

Chen Li is driving a car.

Mr. Pappas is walking.

Mahmood and Ms. Fulana are taking the bus.

Dan is very tired.

He is not going to school.

He is sleeping.

Questions and Answers

		Questions	Answers
1.		Where are all the students going?	They're going to school.
2.		Are Eleni and Susana riding bicycles?	Yes, they are.
3.		Is Chen Li riding a motorcycle?	No, he's driving a car.
4.		Is Mr. Pappas driving?	No, he's walking.
5.		Is Dan going to school?	No, he's sleeping.

Write about the Picture

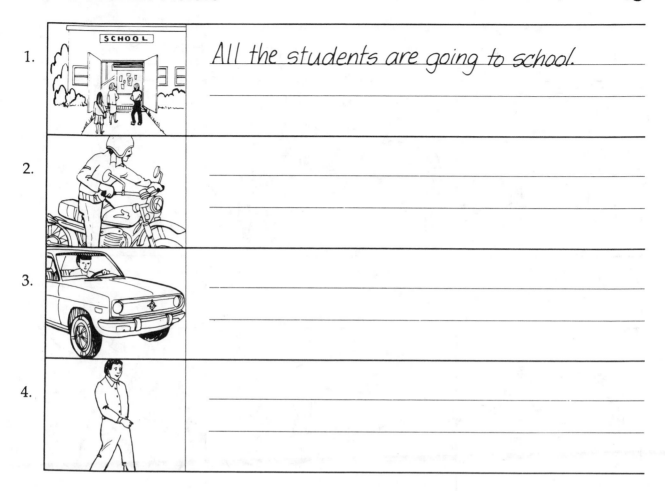

1. _All the students are going to school._

2.

3.

4.

Interaction Grid

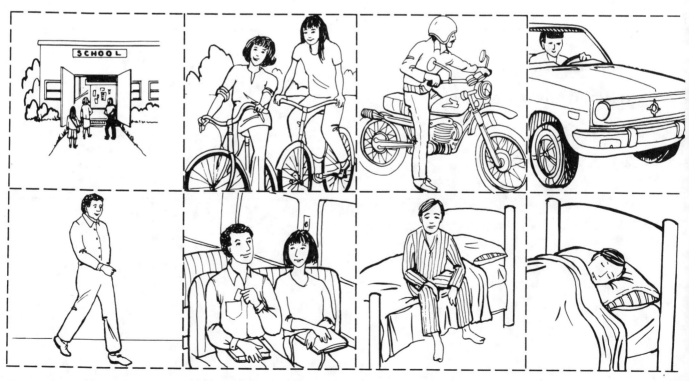

Match the Words and Pictures

car   motorcycle   walking   school
bus   bicycle   sleeping   train

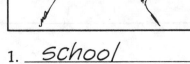

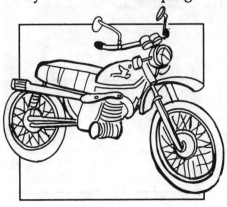

1. _school_

2. _____

3. _____

4. _____

5. _____

6. _____

Write about Yourself

1. How do you go to school?

_____

2. Can you drive a car?

_____

It is unlawful to reproduce this page without express written permission from the Publisher.

8. Taking the Bus

1. Chen Li's car
is not working
this morning

2. is waiting
bus stop

3. bus
is coming

4. is getting on
bus

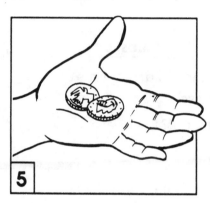

5. is paying
two quarters

6. is sitting down

7. Dan
is running
bus

8. bus
is going

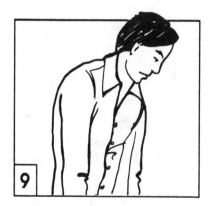

9. missed
bus

1. _____ 2. _____ 3. _____

4. _____ 5. _____ 6. _____

Taking the Bus

Chen Li's car is not working this morning.

He is waiting at the bus stop.

The bus is coming.

He is getting on the bus.

He is paying two quarters.

He is sitting down.

Dan is running for the bus.

The bus is going.

Oh no! He missed the bus!

Questions and Answers

		Questions	Answers
1.		Is Chen Li driving his car to school? Why not?	No, he's not. His car isn't working this morning.
2.		What is he waiting for?	He's waiting for the bus.
3.		Is he getting off the bus?	No, he's getting on.
4.		Is he standing up?	No, he's sitting down.
5.		Is Dan on the bus now?	No, he missed the bus.

Write about the Picture

C

1. *He is waiting at the bus stop.*

2.

3.

4.

Interaction Grid

Permission is granted to make one photocopy of this page in order to do
the **Interaction Grid** *activity and to avoid cutting the page.*

31

Match the Words and Pictures

bus is coming	paying	sitting down	getting on
bus is going	waiting	standing up	getting off

1. _bus is coming_

2. _____

3. _____

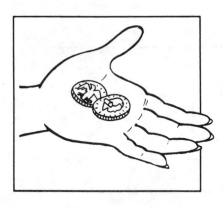

4. _____

5. _____

6. _____

Write about Yourself

1. Do you take the bus sometimes?

_____

2. How much does it cost?

_____

9. A Very Small Classroom

a lot of
students
in
classroom

classroom
very
small

a lot of
students
are sitting
at desks

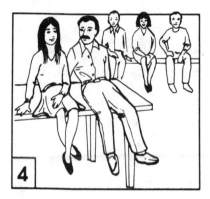

five students
are sitting
on
tables

three students
are sitting
on
carpet

four students
are standing
next to
window

five students
next to
door

a lot of
students

not many
chairs
a big problem

1. _____ 2. _____ 3. _____

4. _____ 5. _____ 6. _____

A Very Small Classroom

A lot of students are in the classroom.

The classroom is very small.

A lot of students are sitting at desks.

Five students are sitting on the tables.

Three students are sitting on the carpet.

Four students are standing next to the window.

Five students are standing next to the door.

A lot of students!

Not many chairs!

It is a big problem!

Questions and Answers

		Questions	Answers
1.		Are a lot of students in the classroom?	Yes—a lot of students.
2.		Is the classroom big?	No, it's small.
3.		How many students are sitting on the tables?	Five.
4.		How many students are standing next to the window?	Four.
5.		How many students are standing next to the door?	Five.

34

Write about the Picture

1. *A lot of students are sitting at desks.*

2.

3.

4.

Interaction Grid

Match the Words and Pictures   D

on the table   in the classroom   next to the desk   next to the table

on the carpet   at the desk   next to the door   a big problem

1. *in the classroom*

2. _____

3. _____

4. _____

5. _____

6. _____

Write about Yourself

1. How many students are in your class today?

_____

2. Where are you sitting?

_____

10. Eleni's Family

1

Eleni

2

mother
father
live
Front Street

3

like to
read
work
garden

4

Eleni's brother
teacher

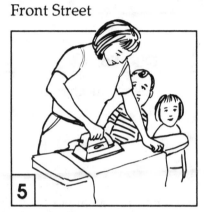

5

wife
is working
at home

6

six children

7

Eleni's sister

8

two children
son and daughter
divorced

9

carpenter

1. _____ 2. _____ 3. _____

4. _____ 5. _____ 6. _____

Eleni's Family

This is Eleni.

This is Eleni's mother and father.

They live with Eleni on Front Street.

They like to read and work in the garden.

This is Eleni's brother. He is a teacher.

His wife is working at home.

They have six children.

This is Eleni's sister.

She has two children—one son and one daughter.

She is divorced.

She is a carpenter.

Questions and Answers

	Questions	Answers
1.	Where do Eleni's mother and father live?	They live on Front Street.
2.	Is Eleni's brother a carpenter?	No, he's a teacher.
3.	Is he married?	Yes, he's married and he has six children.
4.	Is Eleni's sister married?	No, she's divorced and she has two children.
5.	What is her occupation?	She's a carpenter.

Write about the Picture

1. *This is Eleni's mother and father. They live with Eleni on Front Street.*

2.

3.

4.

Interaction Grid

*Permission is granted to make one photocopy of this page in order to do the **Interaction Grid** activity and to avoid cutting the page.*

Match the Words and Pictures

Write your family's names.

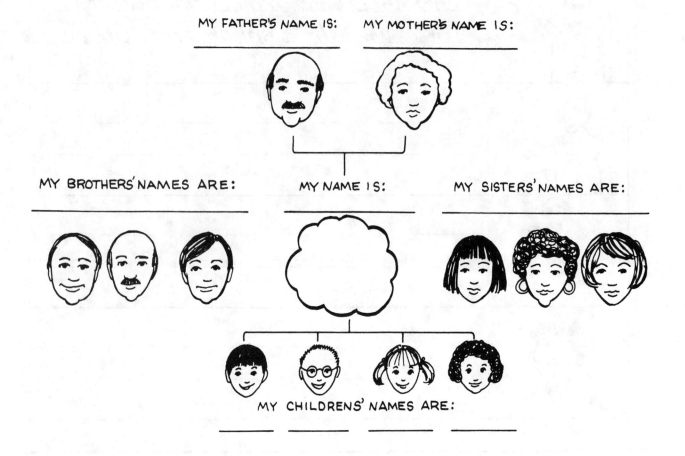

MY FATHER'S NAME IS:

MY MOTHER'S NAME IS:

MY BROTHERS' NAMES ARE:

MY NAME IS:

MY SISTERS' NAMES ARE:

MY CHILDRENS' NAMES ARE:

Write about Yourself

1. How many people are in your family?

_____

2. How many people live with you?

_____

11. Two Brothers

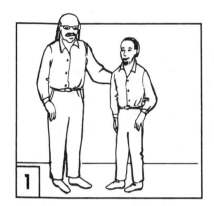

1

two
men
brothers

2

one
tall
other
short

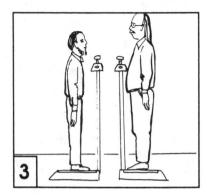

3

one
heavy
other
slender

4

one
long
gray hair

5

other
short
black hair

6

one
mustache
other
beard

7

one wears glasses
other does not

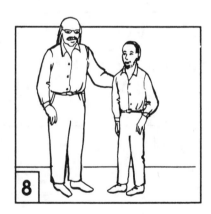

8

are
brothers

9

but
look
different

---

1. _____   2. _____   3. _____

4. _____   5. _____   6. _____

Two Brothers

These two men are brothers.

One brother is tall. The other is short.

One brother is heavy. The other is slender.

One has long gray hair. The other has short black hair.

One has a mustache. The other has a beard.

One brother wears glasses. The other does not.

They are brothers.

But they look different!

Questions and Answers

		Questions	Answers
1.		Are they brothers?	Yes, they are.
2.		Are they tall?	One brother is tall. The other is short.
3.		Are they slender?	One brother is slender. The other is heavy.
4.		Do they both wear glasses?	No, only one brother wears glasses.
5.		Do they look the same?	No! They look different!

42   *It is unlawful to reproduce this page without express written permission from the Publisher.*

Write about the Picture

1. *These two men are brothers.*

2.

3.

4.

Interaction Grid

Match the Words and Pictures

tall   heavy   black hair   beard

short   slender   glasses   mustache

1. _black hair_

2. _____

3. _____

4. _____

5. _____

6. _____

Write about Yourself

What do you look like?

_____

_____

12. Going Downtown

1. Mr. Chaam
is riding
bicycle
downtown

2. is going
bank

3. bank
next to
shoe store

4. is going
drugstore

5. drugstore
across from
park

6. is going
bookstore

7. bookstore
around the corner
post office

8. is going
bakery

9. bakery
down the street
school

---

1. _____ 2. _____ 3. _____

4. _____ 5. _____ 6. _____

Going Downtown

Mr. Chaam is riding his bicycle downtown.

He is going to the bank.

The bank is next to the shoe store.

He is going to the drugstore.

The drugstore is across from the park.

He is going to the bookstore.

The bookstore is around the corner from the post office.

He is going to the bakery.

The bakery is down the street from the school.

Questions and Answers

	Questions	Answers
1.	Is Mr. Chaam driving a car?	No, he's riding a bicycle.
2.	Where is he going?	He's going to the bank.
3.	Where is the drugstore?	It's across from the park.
4.	Where is the bookstore?	It's around the corner from the post office.
5.	Is he going to the hospital?	No, he's not. He's going to the bakery.

Write about the Picture

1. BANK — *He is going to the bank.*

2. BANK / SHOES

3. DRUGSTORE

4. DRUG STORE

Interaction Grid

Match the Words and Pictures

bank   drugstore   post office   school

shoestore   factory   bakery   restaurant

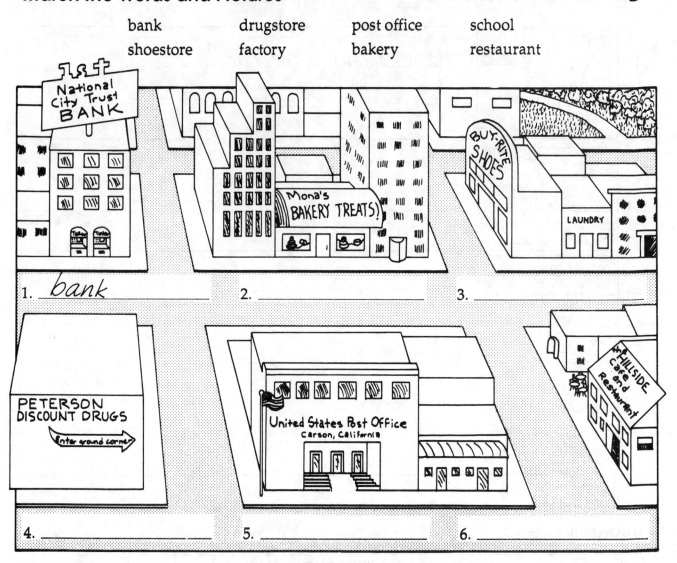

1. *bank*

2. _____

3. _____

4. _____

5. _____

6. _____

Write about Yourself

1. Where are you going?

_____

2. Where is it?

_____

13. A Busy Day

1

6:00
morning
Tomas
is waking up

2

7:30
morning
gas station

3

is buying
gasoline

4

2:15
afternoon
laundromat

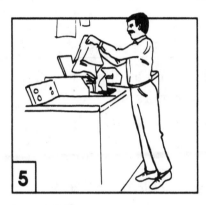

5

is washing
clothes

6

6:45
evening
school

7

is studying
English

8

11:30
at night
home

9

is going
bed
Good night!

1. _____ 2. _____ 3. _____

4. _____ 5. _____ 6. _____

A Busy Day

B

It is 6:00 in the morning. Tomas is waking up.

At 7:30 in the morning, he is at the gas station.

He is buying gasoline.

At 2:15 in the afternoon, he is at the laundromat.

He is washing his clothes.

At 6:45 in the evening, he is at school.

He is studying English.

At 11:30 at night, he is at home.

He is going to bed. Good night!

Questions and Answers

	Questions	Answers
1.	What is Tomas doing at 6:00 in the morning?	He's waking up.
2.	What is he doing at 7:30 in the morning?	He's buying gasoline at the gas station.
3.	What is he doing at 2:15 in the afternoon?	He's washing his clothes at the laundromat.
4.	What is he doing at 6:45 in the evening?	He's studying English at school.
5.	What is he doing at 11:30 at night?	He's going to bed. Good night!

50

Write about the Picture

1. *It is 6:00 in the morning.*
   Tomas is waking up.

2.

3.

4.

Interaction Grid

Match the Words and Pictures
D

gas station   laundromat   school   at home
buying gas   washing clothes   studying   going to bed

1. *gas station*   2. _____   3. _____

4. _____   5. _____   6. _____

Write about Yourself

1. What are you doing at 7:00 in the morning?

_____

2. What are you doing at 11:00 at night?

_____

14. Coming Home from Work

1

6:00
evening
Mrs. Wilson
is coming home

2

works
hospital
nurse

3

is taking off
shoes
uniform

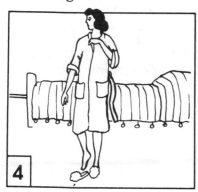

4

is putting on
robe
slippers

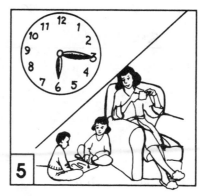

5

6:15
is relaxing
armchair

6

6:30
Mr. Wilson
is coming home
office

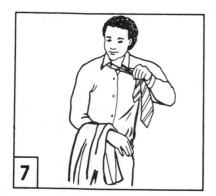

7

is taking off
jacket
tie

8

7:30
is putting on
apron

9

is cooking dinner
tonight
tomorrow night

1. _____ 2. _____ 3. _____

4. _____ 5. _____ 6. _____

Coming Home from Work

It is 6:00 in the evening.

Mrs. Wilson is coming home from work.

She works at the hospital. She is a nurse.

She is taking off her shoes and her uniform.

She is putting on her robe and slippers.

At 6:15, she is relaxing in the armchair.

It is 6:30. Mr. Wilson is coming home from the office.

He is taking off his jacket and tie.

At 7:30, he is putting on an apron in the kitchen.

He is cooking dinner tonight.

Mrs. Wilson is cooking dinner tomorrow night.

Questions and Answers

		Questions	Answers
1.		Is Mrs. Wilson going to work?	No, she's coming home from work.
2.		What is Mrs. Wilson's occupation?	She's a nurse.
3.		What is she taking off?	She's taking off her shoes and her uniform.
4.		What is Mr. Wilson putting on?	He's putting on an apron.
5.		Is Mr. Wilson cooking tonight? When is Mrs. Wilson cooking?	Yes, he is. She's cooking tomorrow night.

54

Write about the Picture

1. It is 6:00 in the evening.
Mrs. Wilson is coming home from work.

2.

3.

4.

Interaction Grid

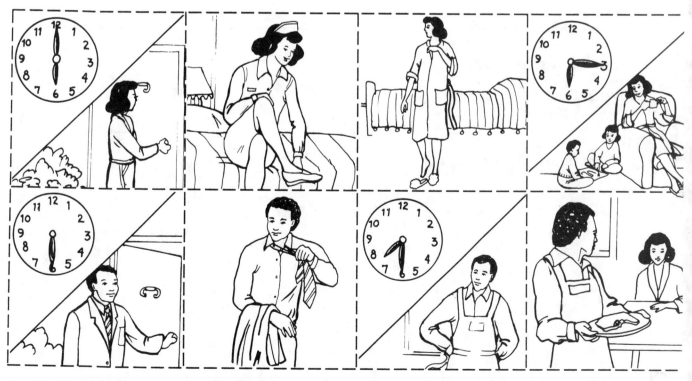

Match the Words and Pictures

shoes   robe   coming home   relaxing

jacket   apron   cooking dinner   working

1. *coming home*   2. _____   3. _____

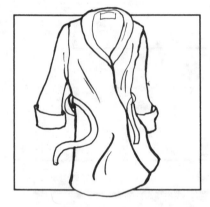  

4. _____   5. _____   6. _____

Write about Yourself

1. What time do you come home?

_____

2. What time do you eat dinner?

_____

15. Home at Night

1
8:00
at night
Mr. Chaam
is relaxing

2
is turning on
lamp
living room

3
is turning on
TV

4
is watching
TV
is drinking
tea

5
now
11:00
sleepy

6
is turning off
TV

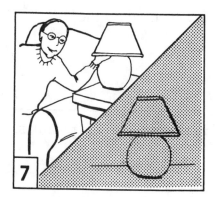

7
is turning off
lamp

8
is putting on
pajamas

9
is going
bed

1. _____ 2. _____ 3. _____

4. _____ 5. _____ 6. _____

Home at Night

It is 8:00 at night. Mr. Chaam is relaxing at home.

He is turning on the lamp in the living room.

He is turning on the TV, too.

He is watching TV and drinking tea.

Now it is 11:00.

He is sleepy now.

He is turning off the TV.

He is turning off the lamp, too.

He is putting on his pajamas.

He is going to bed.

Questions and Answers

		Questions	Answers
1.		What time is it?	It's 8:00 at night.
2.		What is Mr. Chaam watching?	He's watching TV.
3.		What is he turning off?	He's turning off the TV.
4.		What is he putting on?	He's putting on his pajamas.
5.		Is he going to bed? Why?	Yes, he is. He's sleepy.

Write about the Picture

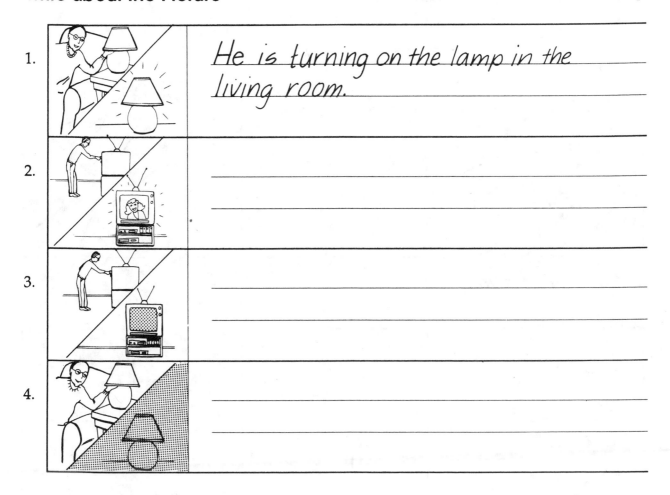

1. *He is turning on the lamp in the living room.*

2.

3.

4.

Interaction Grid

Match the Words and Pictures

lamp   bed   at night   relaxing at home
TV   pajamas   sleepy   drinking tea

1. *relaxing at home*

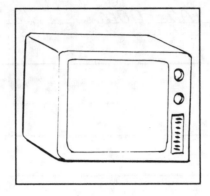

2. _____

3. _____

4. _____

5. _____

6. _____

Write about Yourself

1. Do you watch TV at night?

_____

2. What time do you go to bed?

_____

16. Thinking about Things

1

Mahmood
is thinking about
Ms. Fulana
in love

2

Mr. Chaam
is thinking about
money
worried

3

Chen Li
is thinking about
medicine
sick

4

Dan
is thinking about
family
lonely

5

Eleni
is thinking about
bed
sleepy

6

Mr. and Mrs. Lim
are thinking about
lunch
hungry

7

Susana
is thinking about
new job

8

Tomas
is thinking about
drinking soda

9

Mr. Pappas
is not thinking about
anything

1. _____ 2. _____ 3. _____

4. _____ 5. _____ 6. _____

Mahmood is thinking about Ms. Fulana. He is in love.

Mr. Chaam is thinking about money. He is worried.

Chen Li is thinking about taking some medicine. He is sick.

Dan is thinking about his family in Viet Nam. He is lonely.

Eleni is thinking about her bed. She is sleepy.

Mr. and Mrs. Lim are thinking about lunch. They are hungry.

Susana is thinking about her new job. She is happy.

Tomas is thinking about drinking a soda. He is thirsty.

Mr. Pappas is not thinking about anything. He is bored.

Questions and Answers

		Questions	Answers
1.		What is Dan thinking about? Why?	He's thinking about his family in Viet Nam. He's lonely.
2.		Are Mr. and Mrs. Lim thinking about work? Why?	No, they're thinking about lunch. They're hungry.
3.		Is Susana thinking about her new job?	Yes, she is! She's happy!
4.		What is Tomas thinking about? Why?	He's thinking about drinking a soda. He's thirsty.
5.		What is Mr. Pappas thinking about?	He's not thinking about anything. He's bored.

Write about the Picture

1. *Mahmood is thinking about Ms. Fulana. He is in love.*

2.

3.

4.

Interaction Grid

Match the Words and Pictures   D

job   lunch   boyfriend   medicine
money   soda   family   sleepy

1. *sleepy*

2. _____

3. _____

4. _____

5. _____

6. _____

Write about Yourself

1. What are you thinking about?

_____

2. Why?

_____

17. Moving to a New Apartment

Thursday
9:00
morning

Mr. and Mrs. Lim
are moving
new
apartment

address
624 Washburn Avenue

are carrying
sofa
armchair
living room

are carrying
table
box of dishes
kitchen

are carrying
bed
dresser
bedroom

11:00
at night

very tired

moving
a lot of
work

---

1. _____ 2. _____ 3. _____

4. _____ 5. _____ 6. _____

Moving to a New Apartment

It is Thursday.

It is 9:00 in the morning.

Mr. and Mrs. Lim are moving to a new apartment.

The address is 624 Washburn Avenue.

They are carrying a sofa and an armchair to the living room.

They are carrying a table and a box of dishes to the kitchen.

They are carrying a bed and a dresser to the bedroom.

Now it is 11:00 at night.

They are very tired.

Moving to a new apartment is a lot of work!

Questions and Answers

		Questions	Answers
1.		What are Mr. and Mrs. Lim doing?	They're moving to a new apartment.
2.		What are they carrying? Where?	They're carrying a sofa and an armchair. To the living room.
3.		Where are they carrying the table and the box of dishes?	To the kitchen.
4.		Are they carrying the bed and the dresser to the kitchen?	No. They're carrying them to the bedroom.
5.		Are they tired? Why?	Yes, they are. Moving to a new apartment is a lot of work!

Write about the Picture

1. Mr. and Mrs. Lim are moving to a new apartment.

2.

3.

4.

Interaction Grid

Match the Words and Pictures

| sofa | bed | boxes | dishes |
| armchair | dresser | table | apartment |

1. *dresser*

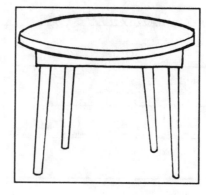

2. _____

3. _____

4. _____

5. _____

6. _____

Write about Yourself

1. Do you live in a house or an apartment?

_____

2. Is your home old or new?

_____

18. Fixing an Old House

1.
Mr. Chaam
is buying
old house
Mission Street

2.
not
good
house

3.
carpenter
is fixing
house

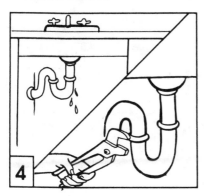

4.
sink
is leaking
is fixing
pipes and faucet

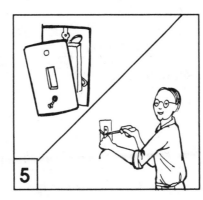

5.
light switch
is not working
is fixing
wires

6.
windows cracked
is putting in
new windows

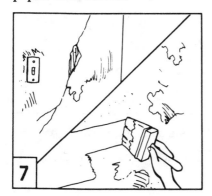

7.
walls
dirty
is painting

8.
stove
broken
is buying

9.
house
beautiful
now

1. _____   2. _____   3. _____

4. _____   5. _____   6. _____

Fixing an Old House

Mr. Chaam is buying an old house on Mission Street.

It is not a good house.

Mr. Chaam is a carpenter. He is fixing the old house.

The sink is leaking. He is fixing the pipes and the faucet.

The light switch is not working. He is fixing the wires.

The windows are cracked. He is putting in new windows.

The walls are dirty. He is painting the walls.

The stove is broken. He is buying a new stove.

The house is beautiful now!

Questions and Answers

	Questions	Answers
1.	Is this a new house?	No, it's an old house.
2.	What is Mr. Chaam doing?	He's fixing the old house.
3.	What is he fixing? Why?	He's fixing the light switch. It's not working.
4.	What is he buying? Why?	He's buying a new stove. The old stove is broken.
5.	Is this a good house now?	Yes, the house is beautiful now!

Write about the Picture

1. The sink is leaking. He is fixing
the pipes and the faucet.

2.

3.

4.

Interaction Grid

Match the Words and Pictures

new house	light switch	walls	stove
old house	pipes	window	sink

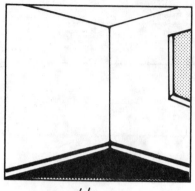

1. __walls__

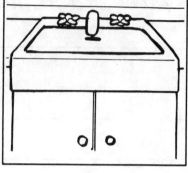

2. _____

3. _____

4. _____

5. _____

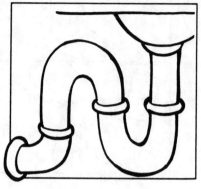

6. _____

Write about Yourself

1. Are you buying or renting your home?

_____

2. Does the stove work in your home?

_____

19. At the Supermarket

Mr. and Mrs. Lim
supermarket

are buying
chicken
$2.29
pound

are buying
coffee
$5.79
can

are buying
eggs
95¢
dozen

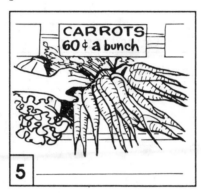

are buying
carrots
60¢
bunch

are buying
rice
$1.40
bag

milk
baby
$1.90 gallon

are paying
checker

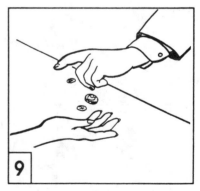

are taking
change

---

1. _____ 2. _____ 3. _____

4. _____ 5. _____ 6. _____

At the Supermarket

Mr. and Mrs. Lim are at the supermarket.

They are buying chicken. Chicken is $2.29 a pound.

They are buying coffee. Coffee is $5.79 a can.

They are buying eggs. Eggs are 95¢ a dozen.

They are buying carrots. Carrots are 60¢ a bunch.

They are buying rice. Rice is $1.40 a bag.

They are buying milk for their baby.

Milk is $1.90 a gallon.

They are paying the checker.

They are taking their change.

Questions and Answers

		Questions	Answers
1.		Where are Mr. and Mrs. Lim?	They're at the supermarket.
2.		What are they buying? How much are they?	They're buying eggs. They're 95¢ a dozen.
3.		What are they buying? How much is it?	They're buying rice. It's $1.40 a bag.
4.		How much is the milk? Who is the milk for?	It's $1.90 a gallon. It's for their baby.
5.		Are they paying the checker?	Yes, they are.

1. *They are buying chicken.*
   Chicken is $2.29 a pound.

2.

3.

4.

Interaction Grid

Match the Words and Pictures

supermarket   rice   banana   chicken

milk   carrots   eggs   coffee

MILK
$1.90
A GALLON

CHICKEN
$2.29
a pound

eggs
95¢
a dozen

1. _milk_

2. _____

3. _____

coffee
$5.79
a can

CARROTS
60¢ a bunch

Rice
$1.40
a bag

4. _____

5. _____

6. _____

Write about Yourself

1. What do you buy at the supermarket?

_____

2. How much does it cost?

_____

20. Buying Clothes for the Children   A

1

Mrs. Wilson
department
store

2

is buying
clothes
two children

3

T-shirts
cheap
$6.95

4

socks
cheap
$2.50

5

pants
expensive
$22.00

6

shoes
expensive
$28.00

7

is taking
clothes
cashier

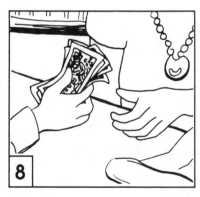

8

is paying
$118.90
a lot of money

9

children
expensive

1. _____   2. _____   3. _____

4. _____   5. _____   6. _____

Buying Clothes for the Children

Mrs. Wilson is in the department store.

She is buying clothes for her two children.

The T-shirts are cheap. They are $6.95.

The socks are cheap. They are $2.50 a pair.

The pants are expensive. They are $22.00.

The shoes are very expensive. They are $28.00 a pair.

She is taking the clothes to the cashier.

She is paying $118.90. Wow! That is a lot of money!

Children are expensive!

Questions and Answers

#		Questions	Answers
1.		Where is Mrs. Wilson?	She's in the department store.
2.		What is she doing?	She's buying clothes for her two children.
3.		Are the socks cheap? How much are they?	Yes, they are. They're $2.50 a pair.
4.		Are the shoes cheap? How much do they cost?	No, they're very expensive. They cost $28.00 a pair.
5.		How much is she paying?	She's paying $118.90. That's a lot of money!

Write about the Picture

1. *Mrs. Wilson is in the department store.*

2.

3.

4.

Interaction Grid

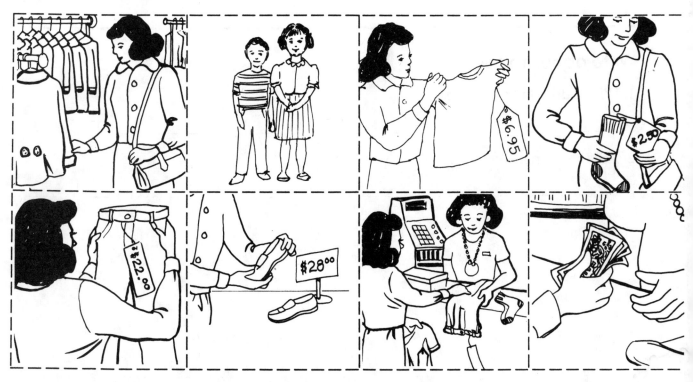

Match the Words and Pictures

D

department store	socks	pants	T-shirt
cashier	shoes	clothes	money

1. _clothes_

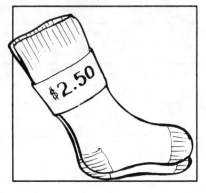

2. _____

3. _____

4. _____

5. _____

6. _____

Write about Yourself

1. Where do you buy clothes?

_____

2. Are they expensive or cheap?

_____

21. Does It Fit?

A

1
Wednesday
afternoon

2
Mrs. Lim
department store

3
is buying
shirt
husband

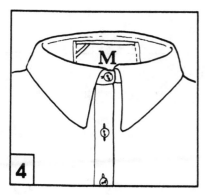

4
shirt
size M—medium

5
Mr. Lim
is trying on
shirt at home
too small

6
Thursday
afternoon
Mrs. Lim
department store

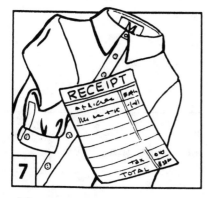

7
shirt
receipt
cashier

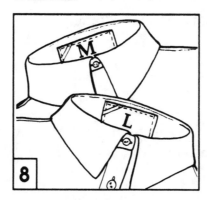

8
is exchanging
shirt
size L—large

9
is trying on
new shirt
fits

1. _____ 2. _____ 3. _____

4. _____ 5. _____ 6. _____

Does It Fit?

It is Wednesday afternoon.

Mrs. Lim is in the department store.

She is buying a shirt for her husband.

The shirt is size M—medium.

Mr. Lim is trying on the shirt at home.

It is too small.

On Thursday afternoon, Mrs. Lim is at the department store again.

She is giving the shirt and the receipt to the cashier.

She is exchanging the shirt for a size L—large.

Mr. Lim is trying on the new shirt.

It fits! He likes it!

Questions and Answers

	Questions	Answers
1.	What is Mrs. Lim doing?	She's buying a shirt in the department store.
2.	What size is the shirt?	It's size M—medium.
3.	What is Mr. Lim doing?	He's trying on the shirt.
4.	What is she giving to the cashier?	She's giving the cashier the shirt and the receipt.
5.	Does this shirt fit?	Yes, it fits! He likes it!

Write about the Picture

1.		*She is buying a shirt for her husband.*
2.		
3.		
4.		

Interaction Grid

Match the Words and Pictures
D

size S—small   size L—large
size M—medium   size XL—extra large

What size are these clothes?

1. *extra large*   2. _____   3. _____   4. _____

1. _____   2. _____   3. _____   4. _____

1. _____   2. _____   3. _____   4. _____

Write about Yourself

1. What size shirt do you wear?

_____

2. What size shoes do you wear?

_____

are shopping
clothes
things
home

shirt
too big
blouse
too small

coffee pot
lamp
nice
likes

bicycle
too expensive

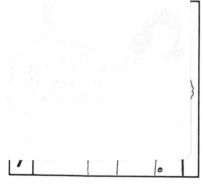

pictures
beautiful

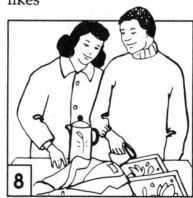

jacket
coffee pot
pictures

$12.00
good deal

1. _____ 2. _____ 3. _____

4. _____ 5. _____ 6. _____

At the Flea Market

The Wilson family is at the flea market.

They are shopping for clothes and things for their home.

This shirt is too big. This blouse is too small.

This jacket is very good. It fits! Mrs. Wilson likes it.

This coffee pot and lamp are nice. Mr. Wilson likes them.

This bicycle is too expensive.

These pictures are beautiful. They like them.

They are buying the jacket, the coffee pot, and the pictures for $12.00.

It is a good deal!

Questions and Answers

		Questions	Answers
1.		Are they at the flea market?	Yes, they are.
2.		What are they shopping for?	They're shopping for clothes and things for their home.
3.		Are the shirt and the blouse good?	No, they're not. One is too big. The other is too small.
4.		Is the jacket good?	Yes, it is. It fits. He likes it.
5.		What are they buying?	They're buying the jacket, the coffee pot, and the pictures.

Write about the Picture

1. *The Wilson family is at the flea market.*

2.

3.

4.

Interaction Grid

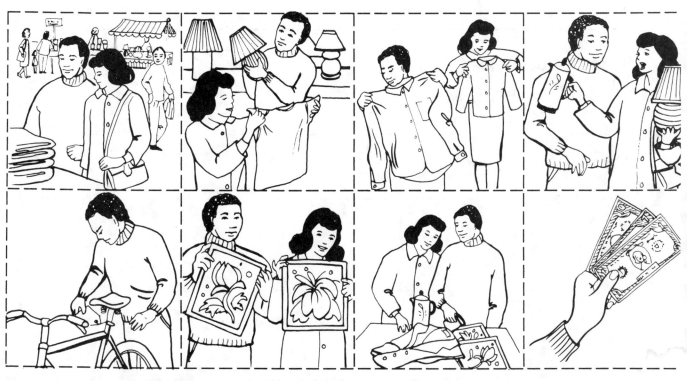

Match the Words and Pictures   D

| flea market | bicycle | coffee pot | shirt |
| jacket | lamp | pictures | blouse |

1. *flea market*

2. _____

3. _____

4. _____

5. _____

6. _____

Write about Yourself

1. Do you shop at a flea market?

_____

2. What do you buy there?

_____

23. Time to Eat

1 Wilson family
at home

2 7:00
in the morning

3 are eating breakfast
eggs
toast
coffee

4 12:30
afternoon

5 are eating lunch
soup
sandwiches
milk

6 6:00
in the evening

7 are eating dinner
fish, rice, and
vegetables

8 9:00
at night

9 are watching TV
snack
popcorn

1. _____ 2. _____ 3. _____

4. _____ 5. _____ 6. _____

Time to Eat

The Wilson family is at home.

It is 7:00 in the morning.

They are eating breakfast—eggs, toast, and coffee.

It is 12:30 in the afternoon.

They are eating lunch—soup, sandwiches, and milk.

It is 6:00 in the evening.

They are eating dinner—fish, rice, and vegetables.

It is 9:00 at night.

They are watching TV.

They are eating a snack—popcorn!

Questions and Answers

	Questions	Answers
1.	Who are they?	They're the Wilson family.
2.	What are they eating at 7:00 in the morning?	They're eating breakfast—eggs, toast, and coffee.
3.	What are they eating at 12:30 in the afternoon?	They're eating lunch—soup, sandwiches, and milk.
4.	What are they eating at 6:00 in the evening?	They're eating dinner—fish, rice, and vegetables.
5.	What are they eating at 9:00 at night?	They're eating a snack—popcorn!

Write about the Picture

1. They are eating breakfast—eggs, toast, and coffee.

2.

3.

4.

Interaction Grid

Match the Words and Pictures

bread   eggs   soup   fish   vegetables

tea   coffee   sandwich   rice   popcorn

1. _vegetables_

2. _____

3. _____

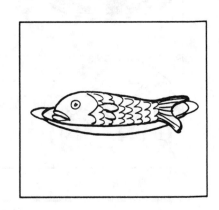

4. _____

5. _____

6. _____

Write about Yourself

1. What do you eat for breakfast?

_____

2. What do you eat for dinner?

_____

24. Going Out to Eat

1

Friday
night

2

is eating out
restaurants

3

Eleni
is ordering
spaghetti and meatballs
Italian food

4

Mr. Pappas
is ordering
vegetables, cheese, fruit
vegetarian food

5

Tomas
is ordering
tacos and beans
Mexican food

6

Susana
is ordering
cheeseburger, fries
chocolate shake

7

Mrs. Lim
is ordering
rice, pork, vegetables

8

Mr. Lim
is ordering
green salad

9

on a diet
Too bad!

1. _____ 2. _____ 3. _____

4. _____ 5. _____ 6. _____

Going Out to Eat

It is Friday night. Everyone is eating out in restaurants.

Eleni is ordering spaghetti and meatballs. She likes Italian food.

Mr. Pappas is ordering vegetables, cheese, and fruit.

He likes vegetarian food.

Tomas is ordering tacos and beans. He likes Mexican food.

Susana is ordering a cheeseburger, fries, and a chocolate shake.

She likes American fast food.

Mrs. Lim is ordering rice, pork, and vegetables.

She likes Chinese food.

Mr. Lim is ordering a small green salad with lemon and a cup of coffee.

He is on a diet! Too bad!

Questions and Answers

		Questions	Answers
1.		What is everyone doing on Friday night?	They're eating out in restaurants.
2.		What is Eleni ordering?	She's ordering spaghetti and meatballs. She likes Italian food.
3.		Is Mr. Pappas ordering cheeseburgers? Why not?	No, he's not. He likes vegetarian food—no meat.
4.		Is Susana ordering a cheeseburger?	Yes, she is. She likes American fast food.
5.		What is Mr. Lim eating? Why?	He's eating a small green salad with lemon. He's on a diet! Too bad!

Write about the Picture

1. Eleni is ordering spaghetti and meatballs. She likes Italian food.

2. _____

3. _____

4. _____

Interaction Grid

Match the Words and Pictures

restaurant   American fast food   Italian food   on a diet
Chinese food   Mexican food   vegetarian food   is ordering

1. *American fast food*   2. _____   3. _____

4. _____   5. _____   6. _____

Write about Yourself

1. What kind of food do you like?

_____

2. What kind of food don't you like?

_____

25. A Day Off

Sunday
many people
are not working
day off

Susana
is riding
park

Tomas
is reading
a book

Mrs. Lim
is visiting
friends

Dan
is walking
park

Eleni
likes
dance

is dancing
disco

Chen Li
likes
dance

is not dancing
is cleaning
apartment

1. _____ 2. _____ 3. _____

4. _____ 5. _____ 6. _____

A Day Off

Today is Sunday.

Many people are not working today. They have the day off.

Susana likes to ride her bicycle on her day off.

She is riding in the park.

Tomas likes to read. He is reading a book.

Mrs. Lim is visiting friends.

Dan is walking in the park.

Eleni likes to dance. She is dancing at the disco.

Chen Li likes to dance, too.

But he is not dancing on his day off.

He is cleaning his apartment.

Questions and Answers

		Questions	Answers
1.		What's Susana doing?	She's riding her bicycle in the park.
2.		What's Tomas doing?	He's reading a book.
3.		What's Eleni doing?	She's dancing at the disco.
4.		Does Chen Li like to dance?	Yes, he does.
5.		Is he dancing?	No, he's cleaning his apartment.

Write about the Picture

1. *Tomas is reading a book.*

2.

3.

4.

Interaction Grid

Match the Words and Pictures

reading   walking   dancing   sleeping

bicycling   jogging   cleaning   drinking

1. _bicycling_

2. _____

3. _____

4. _____

5. _____

6. _____

Write about Yourself

1. What do you like doing on your day off?

_____

2. What don't you like doing?

_____

26. A Bus Trip

1
Ms. Fulana
dressmaker

2
is not working
today
Saturday
day off

3
bus station
is reading
bus schedule

4
is buying
ticket
San Francisco
$11.00

5
is waiting
bus

6
family
is living
San Francisco

7
is going
to see
family

8
is getting on
bus
baby

9
is thinking about
family

---

1. _____ 2. _____ 3. _____

4. _____ 5. _____ 6. _____

A Bus Trip

This is Ms. Fulana. She is a dressmaker.

She is not working today.

It is Saturday. It is her day off.

She is at the bus station.

She is reading the bus schedule.

She is buying a ticket to San Francisco. The ticket costs $11.00.

She is waiting for the bus.

Her family is living in San Francisco now.

She is going to see her family.

She is getting on the bus with her baby.

She is thinking about her family.

Questions and Answers

		Questions	Answers
1.		What is Ms. Fulana's occupation?	She's a dressmaker.
2.		Is she working today? Why not?	No, she's not. Today is Saturday. It's her day off.
3.		Where is she? What's she doing?	She's at the bus station. She's reading the bus schedule.
4.		Where is her family living?	They're living in San Francisco now.
5.		Is she thinking about her work?	No, she's thinking about her family.

Write about the Picture   C

1. She is at the bus station.
   She is reading the bus schedule.

2.

3.

4.

Interaction Grid

Match the Words and Pictures

getting on	bus station	buying a ticket	family
getting off	bus schedule	waiting	baby

1. _bus station_

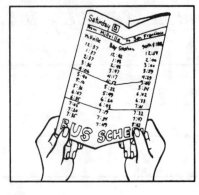

2. _____

3. _____

4. _____

5. _____

6. _____

Write about Yourself

1. Do you take the bus to visit your family?

_____

2. Do you take the bus to visit your friends?

_____

27. Going to the Doctor

Dan
sick

doctor's
office

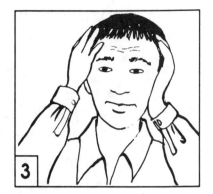

head
aches

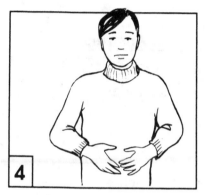

stomach
aches

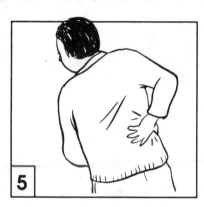

back
hurts

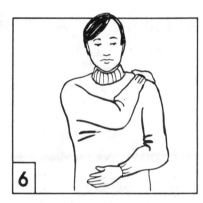

shoulder
hurts

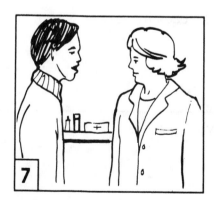

talks
doctor
five minutes

two aspirins
call me
tomorrow

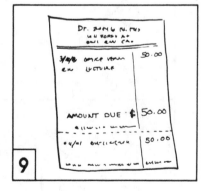

secretary
is saying
$50.00

1. _____ 2. _____ 3. _____

4. _____ 5. _____ 6. _____

It is unlawful to reproduce this page without express written permission from the Publisher.

Going to the Doctor

Dan is sick today.

He is at the doctor's office.

His head aches.

His stomach aches.

His back hurts.

His shoulder hurts.

He talks to the doctor for five minutes.

The doctor is saying, "Take two aspirins and call me tomorrow."

The secretary is saying, "$50.00, please."

Questions and Answers

	Questions	Answers
1.	Is Dan happy?	No, he's not. He's sick today.
2.	What is the problem?	His head aches.
3.	What is the problem?	His back hurts.
4.	Is he talking to the doctor?	Yes, he is.
5.	What is the secretary saying?	She's saying, "$50.00, please."

1. ![head] *His head aches.*

2. ![stomach]

3. ![back]

4. ![shoulder]

Interaction Grid

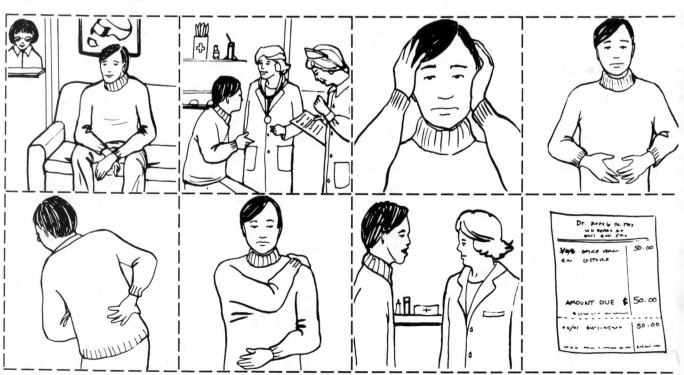

Match the Words and Pictures   D

doctor	head aches	shoulder hurts	ear aches
doctor's office	stomach aches	back hurts	feels great

1. _doctor_

2. _____

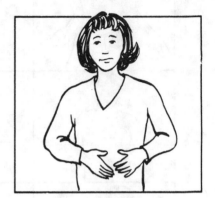

3. _____

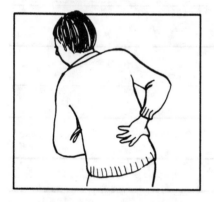

4. _____

5. _____

6. _____

Write about Yourself

How do you feel today?

_____

_____

1

Mahmood
sick

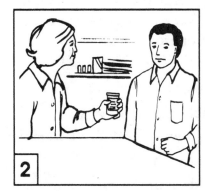

2

is buying
medicine
drugstore
prescription

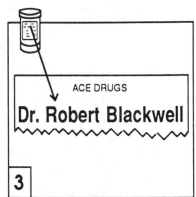

3

doctor's name
Robert Blackwell

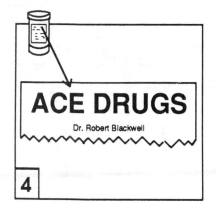

4

drugstore
Ace Drugs

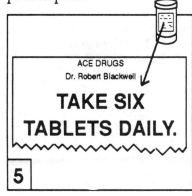

5

is taking
six tablets
every day

6

breakfast
lunch
dinner

7

medicine
sleepy

8

does not drink
alcohol

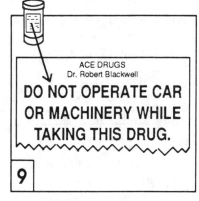

9

does not drive
car
medicine

1. _____ 2. _____ 3. _____

4. _____ 5. _____ 6. _____

Medicine

Mahmood feels sick today.

He is buying medicine at the drugstore.

He has a prescription from the doctor.

The doctor's name is Robert Blackwell.

The drugstore is Ace Drugs.

He is taking six tablets every day.

He takes two tablets with breakfast, two tablets with lunch,
and two tablets with dinner.

This medicine makes him sleepy.

He does not drink alcohol while he is taking this medicine.

He does not drive his car while he is taking this medicine.

Questions and Answers

		Questions	Answers
1.		How does Mahmood feel?	He feels sick.
2.		What is he doing at the drugstore?	He's buying medicine.
3.	**ACE DRUGS** Dr. Robert Blackwell **TAKE SIX TABLETS DAILY.**	How many tablets is he taking every day?	He's taking six tablets every day.
4.	**ACE DRUGS** Dr. Robert Blackwell **DO NOT DRINK ALCOHOL WHILE TAKING THIS DRUG.**	Does he drink alcohol with this medicine?	No, he doesn't!
5.	**ACE DRUGS** Dr. Robert Blackwell **DO NOT OPERATE CAR OR MACHINERY WHILE TAKING THIS DRUG.**	Does he drive a car with this medicine? · Why not?	No, he doesn't! The medicine makes him sleepy!

Write about the Picture

1. *Mahmood feels sick today.*

2. ACE DRUGS
   Dr. Robert Blackwell

3. ACE DRUGS
   Dr. Robert Blackwell
   THESE TABLETS MAY CAUSE DROWSINESS.

4. ACE DRUGS
   Dr. Robert Blackwell
   DO NOT OPERATE CAR OR MACHINERY WHILE TAKING THIS DRUG.

Interaction Grid

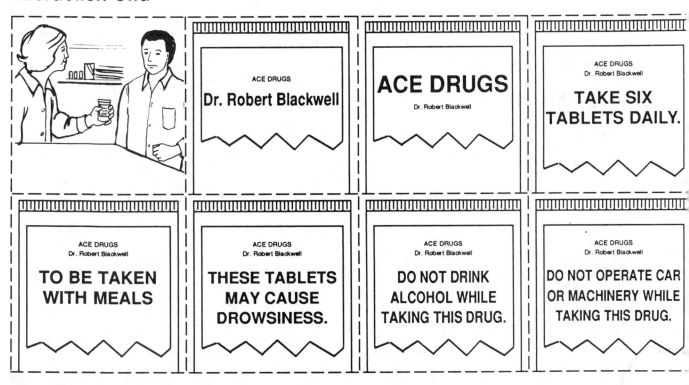

ACE DRUGS
Dr. Robert Blackwell

ACE DRUGS
Dr. Robert Blackwell

ACE DRUGS
Dr. Robert Blackwell
TAKE SIX TABLETS DAILY.

ACE DRUGS
Dr. Robert Blackwell
TO BE TAKEN WITH MEALS

ACE DRUGS
Dr. Robert Blackwell
THESE TABLETS MAY CAUSE DROWSINESS.

ACE DRUGS
Dr. Robert Blackwell
DO NOT DRINK ALCOHOL WHILE TAKING THIS DRUG.

ACE DRUGS
Dr. Robert Blackwell
DO NOT OPERATE CAR OR MACHINERY WHILE TAKING THIS DRUG.

Match the Words and Pictures

don't drive   makes you sleepy   six tablets a day

don't drink   not for children   nine tablets a day

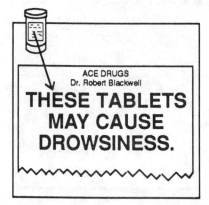

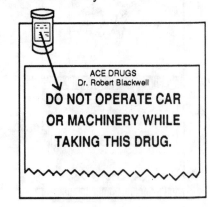

1. *makes you sleepy*　　2. _____　　3. _____

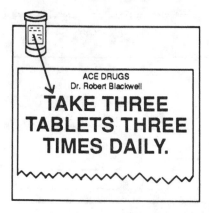

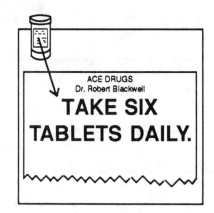

4. _____　　5. _____　　6. _____

Write about Yourself

1. Do you have a doctor?

_____

2. What is your doctor's name?

_____

29. In the Post Office

1

11:30
Wednesday
morning
post office

2

are standing
in line

3

Tomas
is buying
airmail stamps
$6.15

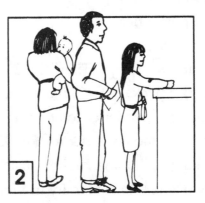

4

Mrs. Lim
is sending
package
$16.00

5

Eleni
is sending
registered letter
$2.10

6

Mr. Pappas
is buying
money order
$10.00

7

Ms. Fulana
is picking up
mail

8

Dan
is sending
two letters

9

a lot of people
crowded

1. _____ 2. _____ 3. _____

4. _____ 5. _____ 6. _____

In the Post Office

It is 11:30 Wednesday morning.

Everyone is in the post office.

They are standing in line.

Tomas is buying airmail stamps. They cost $6.15.

Mrs. Lim is sending a package to China. It costs $16.00.

Eleni is sending a registered letter to Los Angeles. It costs $2.10.

Mr. Pappas is buying a money order for $10.00.

Ms. Fulana is picking up her mail at her post office box.

Dan is sending two letters to his family in Viet Nam.

A lot of people are in the post office this morning.

It is crowded!

Questions and Answers

		Questions	Answers
1.		Where are they? What are they doing?	They're all in the post office. They're standing in line.
2.		What is Tomas doing?	He's buying airmail stamps.
3.		Is Eleni sending a package?	No, she's sending a registered letter to Los Angeles.
4.		Who is buying a money order?	Mr. Pappas.
5.		How many letters is Dan sending to Viet Nam?	He's sending two letters to his family in Viet Nam.

Write about the Picture

1. *It is 11:30 Wednesday morning.*
   Everyone is in the post office.

2.

3.

4.

Interaction Grid

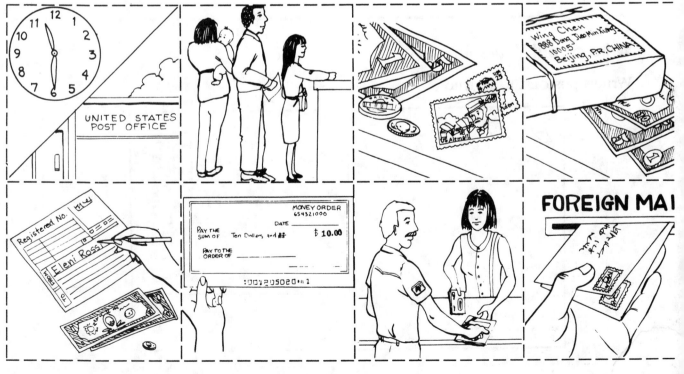

Match the Words and Pictures

stamps   post office   letter   in line

money order   package   airmail   picking up mail

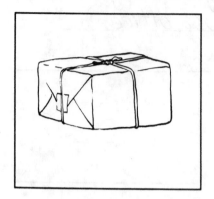

1. _package_

2. _____

3. _____

4. _____

5. _____

6. _____

Write about Yourself

Write a postcard to a friend.

> Dear   ,
>
> PLACE STAMP HERE
>
> _____
>
> _____
>
> Your Friend,   _____

30. At the Bank

A

1

Friday
bank

2

are standing
in line

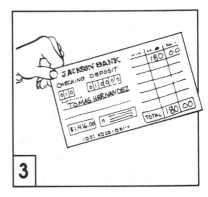

3

Tomas
is depositing $180.00
savings account

4

Mrs. Wilson
is withdrawing
$80.00
new coat

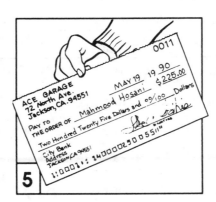

5

Mahmood
is cashing
paycheck
tonight

6

Ms. Fulana
is asking
change
laundromat

7

Mr. Pappas
is buying
traveler's checks

8

Mrs. Lim
is buying
money order

9

Dan
is withdrawing
cash machine

1. _____ 2. _____ 3. _____

4. _____ 5. _____ 6. _____

At the Bank

It is Friday afternoon.

Everyone is at the bank.

They are standing in line.

Tomas is depositing $180.00 in his savings account.

Mrs. Wilson is withdrawing $80.00. She is buying a new coat today.

Mahmood is cashing his paycheck. He is going to a dance tonight.

Ms. Fulana is asking for change. She is going to the laundromat.

Mr. Pappas is buying traveler's checks. He is going on vacation.

Mrs. Lim is buying a money order.

Dan is withdrawing $40.00 from the cash machine.

Questions and Answers

		Questions	Answers
1.		Where are they? What are they doing?	They're at the bank. They're standing in line.
2.		How much is Tomas depositing?	He's depositing $180.00 in his savings account.
3.		Is Mrs. Wilson depositing $80.00? Why?	No, she's not. She's withdrawing $80.00. She's buying a new coat today.
4.		Who is buying traveler's checks? Why?	Mr. Pappas is buying traveler's checks. He's going on vacation.
5.		Is Dan withdrawing money inside the bank?	No, he's outside the bank at the cash machine.

Write about the Picture

1. *It is Friday afternoon.*
   Everyone is at the bank.

2.

3.

4.

Interaction Grid

Match the Words and Pictures

D

withdrawal slip	checkbook	money order	bank
deposit slip	check	traveler's checks	cash machine

1. *deposit slip*

2. _____

3. _____

4. _____

5. _____

6. _____

Write about Yourself

What do you do at the bank?

_____

_____

Vocabulary

Clothing

apron
blouse
clothes
coat
glasses
jacket
pajamas
pants
robe

shirt
shoes
sizes (M—medium, L—large)
slippers
socks
T-shirt
tie
uniform

Countries

China
Greece
Iran
Italy
Mexico
United States
Viet Nam

Descriptive Words and Phrases

beard
beautiful
big
black
bored
broken
busy
cheap
cracked
curly
different
dirty
divorced
expensive

gray
happy
heavy
hungry
in love
large
leaking
lonely
long
married
medium
mustache
new
old

short
sick
single
sleepy
slender
small
straight
sunny
tall
thirsty
tired
worried
young

Expressions

a big problem
a good deal
a pair of
at home
day off
eating out
good night
Happy birthday to you

missed the bus
oh, no
on a diet
one is . . . and the other is . . .
on vacation
too bad
waiting in line
years old

Vocabulary — *continued*

Food/Drink

alcohol	dinner	rice
American fast food	eggs	salad
banana	fish	sandwiches
beans	fruit	snack
breakfast	fries	soda
cake	hamburger	soup
carrots	Italian food	spaghetti
cheese	lemon	tacos
cheeseburger	lunch	tea
Chinese food	Mexican food	toast
chicken	milk	vegetables
chocolate shake	popcorn	vegetarian food
coffee	pork	

Household

armchair	dishes	pipes
barbecue	door	presents (n)
bed	dresser	receipt
bedroom	faucet	sink
book	garden	social security number
box	gasoline	sofa
candles	home	stove
cards	iron	table
carpet	kitchen	telephone
chair	lamp	telephone number
change (money)	light switch	wall
coffee pot	living room	window
cup	money	wires
desk	pictures	

Locatives

across from	in front of
around the corner from	next to
at	on
behind	outside
in	under

Medical

aspirins	nurse
doctor	prescription
drug	sick
drugstore	tablets
medicine	

Vocabulary — *continued*

Occupations

assembler
carpenter
cashier
checker
computer operator
doctor
dressmaker
job

mechanic
nurse
postman
secretary
teacher
TV repairman
waitress

People

baby
boyfriend
brother
child
children
daughter
family
father
friend
grandfather

grandmother
husband
men
mother
neighbor
son
sister
students
wife

Places

address
apartment
bakery
bank
bookstore
bus station
classroom
city
department store
disco

doctor's office
downtown
drugstore
factory
flea market
garage
gas station
high school
home
hospital

house
laundromat
office
park
post office
repair shop
restaurant
school
shoe store
supermarket

Post Office/Bank

airmail stamps
cash machine
check
checkbook
deposit slip
letter
money order

package
paycheck
post office box
registered letter
savings account
traveler's check
withdrawal slip

Vocabulary—*continued*

Pronouns

everyone	she
he	their
her	them
his	we
it	your
my	

Quantities

a lot of	feet
bag	gallon
bunch	inches
can	not many
cup	pair
dozen	pounds

Time Words and Phrases

at night	in the morning
birthday	minutes
day	today
every night	tomorrow
in the afternoon	tonight
in the daytime	
in the evening	

Transportation

bicycle	car
bus	motorcycle
bus schedule	ticket
bus stop	train
bus trip	walking

Vocabulary — *continued*

Verbs

aches
blowing (out)
buying
carrying
cashing
cleaning
coming
cooking
dancing
depositing
drinking
driving
eating
exchanging
feels
fits
fixing
getting (on)
getting (off)
going (to)
has
hurts

laughing
leaking
like, likes
live, lives
looks
missed
moving
ordering
opening
painting
paying
picking (up)
playing
putting (on)
reading
relaxing
riding
running
saying
see
sending

shopping
singing
sitting
sleeping
standing
studying
taking
taking (off)
talking
thinking (about)
trying (on)
turning (on)
turning (off)
visiting
waiting
waking (up)
walking
wears
withdrawing
working

Notes to the Teacher

For whom is this book intended?

The thirty lessons in this book are intended for beginning level students of English as a second or foreign language (ESL or EFL). They are specially designed to assist adult or secondary learners:

- who may have low literacy skills in their primary language,
- who may be unfamiliar with the English alphabet,
- who may be absolute beginners in English, or
- for whom the teacher may not be able to offer explanations or translations in the primary language.

First Class Reader! takes an integrated skills approach to English language development, one that is multimodal in nature to address all learning styles. Because learners are given numerous opportunities to look, listen, speak, read, interact, and write within each *theme-based* lesson, they experience the redundance necessary to understand and to remember. Each lesson is designed to help you, the teacher, provide comprehensible oral and written input for your students without translation. No additional visuals or realia are needed for your students to understand or work with the content.

What themes are explored in this book?

The vocabulary and content of this book may stand alone as a primary classroom text for beginners or serve to complement, review, or reinforce the materials found in any other core grammar or lifeskills text you may be using. The themes revolve around daily life in the United States; the recurring characters are all immigrants. Situations relate to the immigrant experience in general, such as taking a bus, moving to a new apartment, going to work, birthday parties, missing one's family, or shopping at a flea market. Although centered on United States living, all themes are generally relevant to students of EFL, (except perhaps where prices are mentioned in dollars, and procedures for using the bank or post office in America are mentioned). Because the lessons may be used in any order, both ESL and EFL teachers may feel free to select only those lessons that are of interest and relevance to their own particular students.

How does this book address the special needs of low-literacy, orientation-level adult and secondary EFL/ESL students?

1. *First Class Reader!* is heavily illustrated. The concepts and vocabulary used in the book are demonstrated throughout by clear, comprehensible pictures.

2. The book is written almost entirely in the continuous present tense -the verb aspect that is most consistent and easiest to understand. Students are not expected to master complex grammatical sequences while they are developing their literacy skills.

3. Each lesson includes a unique, reading-based *Interaction Grid* activity which gives students the chance to practice their oral language skills and review words and concepts introduced in the reading.

4. Readings are presented in list form (rather than paragraph form) to make it easier for students to follow along.

5. Students are asked to respond to words and phrases by circling, pointing, and copying before seeing them in the context of complete sentence or reading. This is a low-stress way for students to gain familiarity with the printed page and begin developing their literacy skills.

6. Pages are clean, uncluttered, and based upon a consistent format. Students can begin each reading confident that they will not encounter incomprehensible or intimidating instructions on any page.

7. Opportunities are provided in each lesson for learners to work with a partner, offering them the valuable experience of supporting, tutoring, and assisting one another in a non-threatening situation.

8. There is ample repetition of vocabulary in a variety of contexts.

9. Each lesson includes a simple writing activity that enables students to place the words and concepts of the lesson in a personal context. The writing activity can be done individually, in pairs, or in a small group.

What is the format for each lesson?

Each lesson is made up of four pages, labeled A, B, C, and D. The lessons may be presented in any order, according to the immediate needs of the students, or to correspond with lessons in other texts that the class may be using. Each lesson includes the following:

Page A

- nine pictures with key words and phrases printed underneath each picture for students to look at as the teacher reads the story aloud

- a word and phrase recognition activity
- a word and phrase copying activity

Page B
- key words and phrases in the context of a sentence
- the complete story in sentence form to be looked at as the teacher reads again, or to be read aloud with a partner or in groups
- *Questions and Answers*, a partnered oral activity with picture cues for clarification of words and concepts

Page C
- *Write about the Picture*, an activity with picture cues for sentence selection and copying
- *Interaction Grid*, a reading-based oral activity

Page D
- a vocabulary review containing key words and phrases from the reading
- *Match the Words and Pictures*, an activity that reviews words and concepts found in the story and introduces related vocabulary in context.
- *Write about Yourself*, a writing activity intended to relate lesson material to the learner's life

How to Present These Lessons
Page A
1. As students look at the pictures, read the story to them as it appears on page B. Read the sentences slowly, emphasizing key words and concepts. Always read the *picture number* before reading the sentence, to help students focus on the picture you are about to describe. If you have access to an overhead projector, make a transparency of the pictures and point to each picture as you describe it. Permission is hereby granted by the Publisher to make one transparency per instructor for all the classes each session.
2. After reading the entire story to the students (twice, if necessary), read a sentence at random. Then ask student to tell you which picture matches the sentence you have just read. Do this with several sentences, so that students have the chance to check their comprehension.

3. Read words or phrases from page A in random order. Have the students locate the words and phrases and draw a circle around them.
4. Read single words or phrases and have the students copy them on the lines at the bottom of the page.
5. Have the students read words or phrases aloud with a partner, or with you in chorus.

Teaching Tip! It is not necessary to do all of these steps. Do only the ones that you think will help your students, and don't hesitate to invent your own steps!

Page B
1. Read aloud to your students again as they follow along silently or in chorus.
2. Call out key words and phrases again. Have the students locate the words and phrases within the sentence and circle them.
3. Pair up your students. Have partners take turns reading the circled words (and complete sentences, if possible) to each other. As students are working together, you can move around the room, offering encouragement and assistance. Do not worry about pronunciation here. Rather, jot down words and phrases that seem to be giving students trouble and work on these later. In the paired reading, students should be focusing on decoding, comprehension, and peer tutoring. Pronunciation practice is a separate activity and is best done with the whole group at a different time.
4. Practice *Questions and Answers* with your students. At first, they can listen as you model both question and answer. Later, you can read the questions as they supply the answers, and vice versa. If possible, have students cover up the answers with a card and practice responses from memory. You should point out to students that verb forms are written out in the reading (he is, they are) and contracted in *Questions and Answers* (he's, they're).

Teaching Tip! It is not recommended that individual students take turns reading aloud for the class. Performing in front of a group is not conducive to learning to read for either the performer or the listener.

Page C

1. *Write about the Picture.* Ask your students to look at the picture cues and copy the sentence from the story that matches the picture. They can look back at page B for the sentence, or they can write it from memory. You might also write sentence on the blackboard in random order for the students to choose from and copy next to the appropriate picture. When they finish, have them check their page against a partner's and make necessary corrections.

2. To carry out the Interaction Grid activity on page C, it is necessary to photocopy the 8 pictures at the bottom of the page.

Permission is hereby granted by the Publisher to make one photocopy per book for each page C in order to avoid cutting up the book. This permission is granted for a photocopy only and on a one time basis. Handout the photocopies and present the *Interaction Grid* activity , hand out an unmarked 9" x 12" piece of construction paper to each student. Have the students carefully make the grid boards for you, which you will collect and use throughout the term. Ask the students to divide their colored paper into eight equal spaces, using the entire sheet. Magic Markers or crayons are good for this. Have them number the spaces as shown:

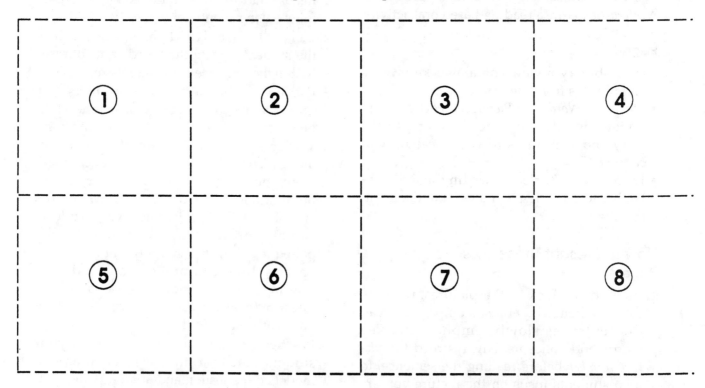

To carry out the *Interaction Grid* activity, each student will need one of these grid boards and a set of eight uncaptioned pictures.

Now hand out the photocopied bottom section of page C. Have students carefully tear or cut the pictures into eight separate "cards." Pair up students and see that each partner has a board and a set of pictures. Stand a file folder on edge between partners so that they cannot look at each other's boards. Student A will take the role of "teacher," and student B will

be the "student." (In this example, let's say that student A is a woman and student B is a man.)

Student A chooses a picture at random from her pile and says a sentence from memory about that picture. She places the picture in space #1 on her grid. Student B looks among his pile for the picture being referred to and places it in space #1 on his grid. This activity continues until all eight of each student's pictures are in place. The partners then remove the file folder to see if their pictures are in the same order. If the pictures are not in the same order, don't worry about it. Students will have another chance when they switch roles, and student B becomes the "teacher."

There will naturally be some confusion about this activity the first time your students do it. Model it carefully with a student or aide in front of the class before beginning pair work with the entire class. After the students have done it once, they will know the routine and carry it out quickly and smoothly on subsequent occasions.

Teaching Tip! This activity is meant to encourage your students to begin working in a manner that is self-directed, cooperative, and fun! Students should not be expected to use perfect grammar or to produce perfect pronunciation. Though it has the appearance of a game and the low-stress feeling of play, *Interaction Grid* work is language acquisition practice with a capital "L."

Page D

1. The illustrations in *Match the Words and Pictures* review vocabulary and phrases from the reading on page B. First, review the words printed at the top of the page with your students. Next, ask students to find the words or phrases that match the pictures below. Finally, ask your students to copy the matching word or phrase on the line underneath each picture.

1. *mechanic*

You might also dictate these words or phrases and have students write them under the appropriate pictures. Students can work alone, in pairs, or in a group.

2. *Write about Yourself.* This activity gives students the chance to apply to their own lives some of the language they have learned. Read the questions aloud as the students follow along. Make sure that the students understand the vocabulary and meaning of each question, then ask them to practice the questions and answers with a partner before they write. Finally, ask students to write the answers to each question. While some students will be prepared, even impatient, to begin writing, others will appreciate the chance to practice questions orally before marking the page.

Teaching Tip! Questions in *Write about Yourself* can be answered with a full sentence, a fragment, or just a single word. Work with your students to decide what level of grammatical complexity is appropriate for your class.